To:

_____

From:

_____

Message:

_____

_____

_____

Grace Notes
for Women

Artwork by Amylee Weeks

CHRISTIAN ART PUBLISHERS

GraceNotes for Women Promise Book

Published by Christian Art Publishers

PO Box 1599, Vereeniging, 1930, RSA

© 2020
First edition 2020

Designed by Christian Art Publishers

Cover designed by Christian Art Publishers

Artwork © Amylee Weeks

Scripture quotations are taken from the Contemporary English Version ©
1991, 1992, 1995 by American Bible Society. Used by permission.

Scripture quotations are taken from the *Holy Bible*, New International
Version®, NIV® Copyright © 1973, 1978, 1984, 2011 by Biblica, Inc.®
Used by permission. All rights reserved worldwide.

Scripture quotations are taken from the *Holy Bible*, New Living Translation,
copyright © 1996, 2004, 2015 by Tyndale House Foundation.
Used by permission of Tyndale House Publishers, Inc., Carol Stream, Illinois
60188. All rights reserved.

Scripture quotations are taken from the New King James Version®. Copyright
© 1982 by Thomas Nelson. Used by permission. All rights reserved.

Scripture quotations are taken from the Holy Bible, English Standard
Version®. ESV® Text Edition: 2016. Copyright © 2001 by Crossway, a
publishing ministry of Good News Publishers. Used by permission. All rights
reserved.

Printed in China

ISBN 978-1-4321-3150-0

Contents

GraceNotes of Joy

GraceNotes of Peace

GraceNotes of Blessing

GraceNotes of Thanksgiving

GraceNotes of Praise

GraceNotes of Salvation

GraceNotes of Encouragement

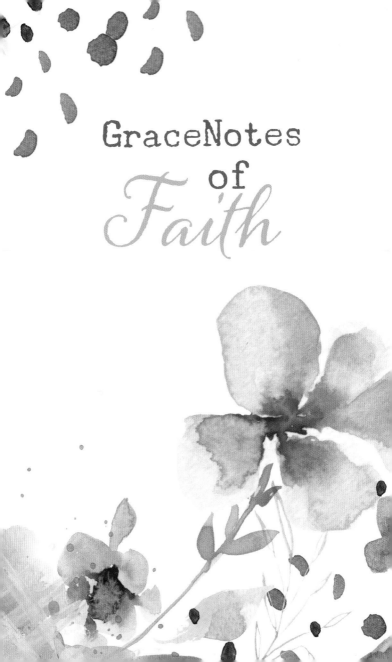

GraceNotes
of
Faith

"I tell you the truth, if you had faith
even as small as a mustard seed,
you could say to this mountain,
'Move from here to there,' and it would move.
Nothing would be impossible."

MATTHEW 17:20

Now faith is the substance of things hoped for,
the evidence of things not seen.

HEBREWS 11:1

We live by faith, not by sight.

2 CORINTHIANS 5:7

For in the gospel the righteousness
of God is revealed – a righteousness
that is by faith from first to last, just as it is
written: "The righteous will live by faith."

ROMANS 1:17

In all circumstances take up the shield of faith,
with which you can extinguish
all the flaming darts of the evil one.

EPHESIANS 6:16

Faith comes from hearing the message,
and the message is heard
through the word about Christ.

ROMANS 10:17

Without faith it is impossible to please Him,
for he who comes to God must believe
that He is, and that He is a rewarder
of those who diligently seek Him.

HEBREWS 11:6

Jesus said, "All things are possible
for one who believes."

MARK 9:23

Be on your guard;
stand firm in the faith;
be courageous; be strong.

1 CORINTHIANS 16:13

Because of Christ
and our faith in Him,
we can now come boldly
and confidently into God's presence.

EPHESIANS 3:12

For I can do everything
through Christ,
who gives me strength.

PHILIPPIANS 4:13

Faith is to
BELIEVE
what we do not
see, and the
reward of this
faith is to see
what we believe.

ST. AUGUSTINE

Blessed is the one who trusts in the LORD,
whose confidence is in Him.

JEREMIAH 17:7

The LORD is good,
a refuge in times of trouble.
He cares for those who trust in Him.

NAHUM 1:7

Trust in the LORD forever,
for the LORD GOD is an everlasting rock.

ISAIAH 26:4

Some trust in chariots and some in horses,
but we trust in the name of the LORD our God.

PSALM 20:7

Those who trust in the Lord will find
new strength. They will soar high on wings
like eagles. They will run and not grow weary.
They will walk and not faint.

ISAIAH 40:31

Trust in the Lord with all your heart
and lean not on your own understanding;
in all your ways acknowledge Him,
and He will make your paths straight.

PROVERBS 3:5-6

Those who know Your name trust in You,
for You, Lord, have never forsaken
those who seek You.

PSALM 9:10

It is better to take refuge in
the Lord than to trust in people.

PSALM 118:8

Blessed is the one
who trusts in the LORD.

PSALM 40:4

The fear of man brings a snare,
but whoever trusts in the LORD shall be safe.

PROVERBS 29:25

Those who listen to instruction will prosper;
those who trust the LORD will be joyful.

PROVERBS 16:20

Put your trust in the LORD.

PSALM 4:5

Christ will always
accept the FAITH
that puts its
trust in Him.

Andrew Murray

I press on toward the goal
to win the prize
for which God has called me
heavenward in Christ Jesus.

PHILIPPIANS 3:14

Take up your positions;
stand firm and see the deliverance
the LORD will give you.

2 CHRONICLES 20:17

Let us throw off everything that hinders
and the sin that so easily entangles.
And let us run with perseverance
the race marked out for us.

HEBREWS 12:1

Blessed is the one who perseveres
under trial because, having stood the test,
that person will receive the crown of life
that the Lord has promised
to those who love Him.

JAMES 1:12

Let us not become weary
in doing good, for at
the proper time we will reap
a harvest if we do not give up.

GALATIANS 6:9

Be strong and do not give up,
for your work will be rewarded.

2 CHRONICLES 15:7

"He who endures to the end shall be saved."

MATTHEW 24:13

Patient endurance is what you need now,
so that you will continue to do God's will.
Then you will receive all
that He has promised.

HEBREWS 10:36

I have fought the good fight,
I have finished the race,
I have kept the faith.

2 TIMOTHY 4:7

Consider it pure joy
whenever you face trials
of many kinds,
because you know
that the testing
of your faith
produces perseverance.

JAMES 1:2-3

Never give up,
for that is
just
the place
and time that the
tide will turn.

Harriet Beecher Stowe

GraceNotes
of
Hope

Blessed are those whose hope
is in the LORD their God.

PSALM 146:5

We have this hope as an anchor for the soul,
firm and secure. It enters the inner sanctuary
behind the curtain, where our forerunner,
Jesus, has entered on our behalf.

HEBREWS 6:19-20

Hope will not lead to disappointment.
For we know how dearly God loves us,
because He has given us the Holy Spirit
to fill our hearts with His love.

ROMANS 5:5

Hope in the LORD!
For with the LORD there is steadfast love,
and with Him is plentiful redemption.

PSALM 130:7

The eye of the LORD is on those who fear Him,
on those who hope in His steadfast love.

PSALM 33:18

Hope deferred makes the heart sick,
but a dream fulfilled is a tree of life.

PROVERBS 13:12

The LORD is good to those whose hope
is in Him, to the one who seeks Him.

LAMENTATIONS 3:25

For everything that was written in the past
was written to teach us, so that through
endurance and the encouragement
of the Scriptures we might have hope.

ROMANS 15:4

God will never forget the needy;
the hope of the afflicted will never perish.

PSALM 9:18

Hope that is seen is not hope;
for why does one still hope for what he sees?
But if we hope for what we do not see,
we eagerly wait for it with perseverance.

ROMANS 8:24-25

GOD is the only
one who can make
the valley of
trouble a door
of
hope.

Catherine Marshall

When doubts filled my mind,
Your comfort gave me renewed hope and cheer.

PSALM 94:19

The LORD comforts His people
and will have compassion on His afflicted ones.

ISAIAH 49:13

"As a mother comforts her child,
so will I comfort you."

ISAIAH 66:13

Praise be to the God and Father of our Lord
Jesus Christ, the Father of compassion
and the God of all comfort,
who comforts us in all our troubles.

2 CORINTHIANS 1:3-4

"I, yes I, am the one who comforts you.
So why are you afraid?"

ISAIAH 51:12

"Blessed are those who mourn,
for they will be comforted."

MATTHEW 5:4

Let Your unfailing love comfort me,
just as You promised me.

PSALM 119:76

Even though I walk through the darkest valley,
I will fear no evil, for You are with me;
Your rod and Your staff, they comfort me.

PSALM 23:4

A Comforting Hope

You, O Lord, help and comfort me.

PSALM 86:17

The Lord is close to the brokenhearted
and saves those who are crushed in spirit.

PSALM 34:18

He heals the brokenhearted
and bandages their wounds.

PSALM 147:3

Just as we share abundantly
in the sufferings of Christ,
so also our comfort abounds through Christ.

2 CORINTHIANS 1:5

Thanks

be to God,
not only for rivers
of ENDLESS JOYS
above, but for
rills of comfort
here below.

Adoniram Judson

GraceNotes
of
Love

"For God so loved the world
that He gave His one and only Son,
that whoever believes in Him
shall not perish but have eternal life."

JOHN 3:16

"As the Father loved Me, I also have
loved you; abide in My love.
If you keep My commandments, you will abide
in My love, just as I have kept My Father's
commandments and abide in His love."

JOHN 15:9-10

I am convinced that neither death nor life, neither
angels nor demons, neither the present nor the
future, nor any powers, neither height nor depth,
nor anything else in all creation, will be able to
separate us from the love of God that is
in Christ Jesus our Lord.

ROMANS 8:38-39

We are more than conquerors
through Him who loved us.

ROMANS 8:37

"I have loved you with an everlasting love;
I have drawn you with unfailing kindness."

JEREMIAH 31:3

Behold what manner of love
the Father has bestowed on us,
that we should be called children of God!

1 JOHN 3:1

The LORD is good and
His love endures forever;
His faithfulness continues
through all generations.

PSALM 100:5

"I lavish unfailing love for
a thousand generations on those
who love Me and obey My commands."

DEUTERONOMY 5:10

This is love: not that we loved God,
but that He loved us and sent His Son
as an atoning sacrifice for our sins.

1 JOHN 4:10

Give thanks to the LORD, for He is good;
His love endures forever.

PSALM 106:1

"A new commandment I give to you,
that you love one another:
just as I have loved you,
you also are to love one another."

JOHN 13:34

By
THE CROSS
we know the
gravity of sin
& the greatness
of God's
love
toward us.

St. Chrysostom

You are a forgiving God,
gracious and compassionate,
slow to anger and abounding in love.

NEHEMIAH 9:17

Through the LORD's mercies
we are not consumed,
because His compassions fail not.

LAMENTATIONS 3:22

The Lord is full of compassion and mercy.

JAMES 5:11

He has made His wonderful works
to be remembered; the LORD is gracious
and full of compassion.

PSALM 111:4

The Lord is good to everyone.
He showers compassion on all His creation.

PSALM 145:9

As a father has compassion
on his children, so the Lord
has compassion on those who fear Him.

PSALM 103:13

May I never forget the good things He does for me.
He forgives all my sins and heals all my diseases.
He redeems me from death and crowns me
with love and tender mercies.

PSALM 103:2-4

Return to the Lord your God,
for He is gracious and merciful,
slow to anger, and of great kindness.

JOEL 2:13

Once again You will have
compassion on us.

MICAH 7:19

He tends His flock like a shepherd:
He gathers the lambs in His arms
and carries them close to His heart.

ISAIAH 40:11

The LORD your God is gracious and merciful.
If you return to Him, He will not continue
to turn His face from you.

2 CHRONICLES 30:9

You, Lord, are a compassionate
and gracious God, slow to anger,
abounding in love and faithfulness.

PSALM 86:15

40

Man may
dismiss
compassion
from his
heart,
but
God never will.
William Cowper

If we love each other,
God lives in us,
and His love is brought
to full expression in us.

1 JOHN 4:12

Love each other deeply,
because love covers
over a multitude of sins.

1 PETER 4:8

"Love your neighbor as yourself."

MATTHEW 19:19

"Love each other as I have loved you."

JOHN 15:12

Love one another deeply, from the heart.

1 PETER 1:22

Pursue righteousness, faith, love and peace.

2 TIMOTHY 2:22

Beloved, if God so loved us,
we also ought to love one another.

1 JOHN 4:11

Love is patient, love is kind. It does not envy,
it does not boast, it is not proud.
It always protects, always trusts,
always hopes, always perseveres.
Love never fails.

1 CORINTHIANS 13:4, 7-8

Let all that you do be done with love.

1 CORINTHIANS 16:14

Whoever does not love
does not know God,
because God is love.

1 JOHN 4:8

"I am giving you a new commandment:
Love each other. Just as I have loved you,
you should love each other.
Your love for one another will prove
to the world that you are My disciples."

JOHN 13:34-35

We love because He first loved us.

1 JOHN 4:19

To *love* someone means to see him as God intended him.

Fyodor Dostoevsky

GraceNotes
of
Joy

The joy of the Lord
is your strength.

NEHEMIAH 8:10

Those who sow with tears
will reap with songs of joy.

PSALM 126:5

"Be happy! Yes, leap for joy!
For a great reward awaits you in heaven."

LUKE 6:23

You turned my wailing into dancing;
You removed my sackcloth
and clothed me with joy.

PSALM 30:11

Those who look to Him for help
will be radiant with joy; no shadow
of shame will darken their faces.

PSALM 34:5

The precepts of the LORD are right,
giving joy to the heart. The commands
of the LORD are radiant, giving light to the eyes.

PSALM 19:8

Honor and majesty are before Him;
strength and gladness are in His place.

1 CHRONICLES 16:27

Light shines on the godly,
and joy on those whose hearts are right.

PSALM 97:11

The LORD has done great things for us,
and we are filled with joy.

PSALM 126:3

A cheerful heart is good medicine,
but a crushed spirit dries up the bones.

PROVERBS 17:22

The kingdom of God is not a matter of eating
and drinking, but of righteousness,
peace and joy in the Holy Spirit.

ROMANS 14:17

Joy

is the serious
business
OF HEAVEN.
C. S. Lewis

Rejoice in the Lord always.

PHILIPPIANS 4:4

Rejoice in the LORD and be glad,
all you who obey Him! Shout for joy,
all you whose hearts are pure!

PSALM 32:11

Glory in His holy name; let the hearts of those
who seek the LORD rejoice! Seek the LORD
and His strength; seek His presence continually!

PSALM 105:3-4

In Him our hearts rejoice, for we trust
in His holy name. Let Your unfailing love
surround us, LORD, for our hope is in You alone.

PSALM 33:21-22

"Rejoice because your names
are written in heaven."

LUKE 10:20

This is the day that the LORD has made;
let us rejoice and be glad in it.

PSALM 118:24

Let all those who seek You rejoice and
be glad in You; let such as love Your salvation
say continually, "The LORD be magnified!"

PSALM 40:16

My heart rejoices in the LORD. There is no one holy
like the LORD; there is no one besides You;
there is no Rock like our God.

1 SAMUEL 2:1-2

May the righteous be glad and rejoice
before God; may they be happy and joyful.

PSALM 68:3

Rejoice with those who rejoice,
and weep with those who weep.

ROMANS 12:15

Rejoice always, pray without ceasing,
give thanks in all circumstances;
for this is the will of God in Christ Jesus for you.

1 THESSALONIANS 5:16-18

When you cannot
REJOICE in
feelings,
circumstances
or conditions,
rejoice in the
Lord.
A. B. Simpson

GraceNotes
of
Peace

The LORD gives strength to His people;
the LORD blesses His people with peace.

PSALM 29:11

"Peace I leave with you; My peace I give you. Do not let
your hearts be troubled and do not be afraid."

JOHN 14:27

In peace I will lie down and sleep, for You alone, LORD,
make me dwell in safety.

PSALM 4:8

The work of righteousness will be peace, and the effect
of righteousness, quietness and assurance forever.

ISAIAH 32:17

"In Me you may have peace. In the world you will have tribulation. But take heart; I have overcome the world."

JOHN 16:33

LORD, You will grant us peace; all we have accomplished is really from You.

ISAIAH 26:12

Let the peace of Christ rule in your hearts, since as members of one body you were called to peace.

COLOSSIANS 3:15

"My people will dwell in a peaceful habitation, in secure dwellings, and in quiet resting places."

ISAIAH 32:18

The Gift of Peace

Because of God's tender mercy, the morning light
from heaven is about to break upon us,
to guide us to the path of peace.

LUKE 1:78-79

Great peace have those who love Your law,
and nothing can make them stumble.

PSALM 119:165

God is not a God of confusion but of peace.

1 CORINTHIANS 14:33

When a man's ways please the Lᴏʀᴅ, He makes even
his enemies to be at peace with him.

PROVERBS 16:7

God can work
peace
through
us only if
He has worked
PEACE in us ...
Those in the worst
of circumstances
but with God need
NEVER LACK PEACE.

John MacArthur

Those who live in the shelter of the Most High
will find rest in the shadow of the Almighty.

PSALM 91:1

The Lord replied, "My Presence
will go with you, and I will give you rest."

EXODUS 33:14

Jesus said, "Come to Me, all of you
who are weary and carry heavy burdens,
and I will give you rest. Take My yoke upon you.
Let Me teach you, because I am humble
and gentle at heart, and you will
find rest for your souls."

MATTHEW 11:28-30

He said to them, "Come away by yourselves
to a desolate place and rest a while."

MARK 6:31

Rest in the LORD, and wait patiently for Him;
do not fret because of him who prospers
in his way, because of the man
who brings wicked schemes to pass.

PSALM 37:7

This is what the Sovereign LORD says:
"Only in returning to Me and resting in Me
will you be saved. In quietness
and confidence is your strength."

ISAIAH 30:15

The fear of the LORD leads to life;
then one rests content, untouched by trouble.

PROVERBS 19:23

My soul finds rest in God;
my salvation comes from Him.

PSALM 62:1

Rest for Your Soul

There is a special rest still waiting
for the people of God. For all who have
entered into God's rest have rested from their labors,
just as God did after creating the world.

HEBREWS 4:9-10

In vain you rise early and stay up late,
toiling for food to eat – for He grants sleep
to those He loves.

PSALM 127:2

"Six days you shall labor,
but on the seventh day you shall rest."

EXODUS 34:21

You have created
us for Yourself,
and our HEART is
not quiet until
it rests in You.

St. Augustine

Be strong, and do not fear, for your God
is coming to destroy your enemies.
He is coming to save you.

ISAIAH 35:4

Commit everything you do to the LORD.
Trust Him, and He will help you.

PSALM 37:5

"So do not fear, for I am with you;
do not be dismayed, for I am your God."

ISAIAH 41:10

The LORD is my light and my salvation;
whom shall I fear? The LORD is the strength
of my life; of whom shall I be afraid?

PSALM 27:1

Do not be anxious about anything,
but in every situation, by prayer and petition,
with thanksgiving, present your requests to God.
And the peace of God, which transcends all
understanding, will guard your hearts
and your minds in Christ Jesus.

PHILIPPIANS 4:6-7

I have set the LORD always before me.
Because He is at my right hand, I will not be shaken.

PSALM 16:8

Do not be afraid and do not panic before them.
For the LORD your God will personally go ahead of you.
He will neither fail you nor abandon you.

DEUTERONOMY 31:6

Cast all your anxiety on Him
because He cares for you.

1 PETER 5:7

No Need to Fear

"Do not be anxious about how you should
defend yourself or what you should say,
for the Holy Spirit will teach you in
that very hour what you ought to say."

LUKE 12:11-12

"Therefore do not be anxious about tomorrow,
for tomorrow will be anxious for itself.
Sufficient for the day is its own trouble."

MATTHEW 6:34

Anxiety weighs down the heart,
but a kind word cheers it up.

PROVERBS 12:25

Do not be afraid or discouraged, for the LORD will
personally go ahead of you. He will be with you;
He will neither fail you nor abandon you.

DEUTERONOMY 31:8

Anxiety does not
empty tomorrow
of its sorrows,
but only empties
today of

its
strength.

Charles H. Spurgeon

GraceNotes
of
Blessing

The blessing of the LORD brings wealth,
without painful toil for it.

PROVERBS 10:22

"Blessed are those who hunger
and thirst for righteousness,
for they shall be satisfied."

MATTHEW 5:6

May you be blessed by the LORD,
the Maker of heaven and earth.

PSALM 115:15

Blessed are those whose way is blameless,
who walk in the law of the LORD!

PSALM 119:1

Oh, taste and see that the LORD is good;
blessed is the man who trusts in Him!

PSALM 34:8

The LORD will indeed give what is good,
and our land will yield its harvest.

PSALM 85:12

When You open Your hand, You satisfy
the hunger and thirst of every living thing.
The LORD is righteous in everything
He does; He is filled with kindness.

PSALM 145:16-17

"Bring all the tithes into the storehouse
so there will be enough food
in My Temple. If you do," says the LORD
of Heaven's Armies, "I will open the windows
of heaven for you. I will pour out a blessing
so great you won't have enough room
to take it in! Try it! Put Me to the test!"

MALACHI 3:10

"The LORD bless you and keep you;
the LORD make His face shine upon you,
and be gracious to you; the LORD lift up His
countenance upon you, and give you peace. "

NUMBERS 6:24-26

All praise to God, the Father of our Lord
Jesus Christ, who has blessed us
with every spiritual blessing in the heavenly
realms because we are united with Christ.

EPHESIANS 1:3

The LORD your God will bless you
in all your harvest and in all the work of
your hands, and your joy will be complete.

DEUTERONOMY 16:15

To LOVE
God is the
greatest
of virtues;
to be loved by
God is the
greatest of
BLESSINGS.

Daily Provision

"Your Father knows
what you need before you ask Him."

MATTHEW 6:8

He provides food for those who fear Him;
He remembers His covenant forever.

PSALM 111:5

God shall supply all your need according
to His riches in glory by Christ Jesus.

PHILIPPIANS 4:19

"Give, and it will be given to you.
A good measure, pressed down, shaken
together and running over, will be poured
into your lap. For with the measure you use,
it will be measured to you."

LUKE 6:38

Daily Provision

"Seek the Kingdom of God above all else,
and live righteously, and He will give you
everything you need."

MATTHEW 6:33

"Consider the ravens, for they neither sow nor reap,
which have neither storehouse nor barn;
and God feeds them. Of how much more
value are you than the birds?"

LUKE 12:24

The lions may grow weak and hungry, but
those who seek the LORD lack no good thing.

PSALM 34:10

The LORD is my shepherd;
I have all that I need.

PSALM 23:1

He will give the rain
for your land in its season,
the early rain and the later rain,
that you may gather in your grain
and your wine and your oil.
And He will give grass
in your fields for your livestock,
and you shall eat and be full.

DEUTERONOMY 11:14-15

He who supplies seed to the sower
and bread for food will also supply
and increase your store of seed
and will enlarge the harvest
of your righteousness.

2 CORINTHIANS 9:10

God doesn't **PROMISE** to overflow your bank account, but

promises to **PROVIDE** for your every need.

Paul Chappell

We have different gifts,
according to the grace given to each of us.
If your gift is prophesying, then prophesy in
accordance with your faith; if it is serving,
then serve; if it is teaching, then teach ...

ROMANS 12:6-7

God has given each of you a gift
from His great variety of spiritual gifts.
Use them well to serve one another.

1 PETER 4:10

There are different kinds of gifts,
but the same Spirit distributes them.
There are different kinds of service,
but the same Lord.

1 CORINTHIANS 12:4-5

Fan into flame the gift of God.
For the Spirit God gave us does not make us timid,
but gives us power, love and self-discipline.

2 TIMOTHY 1:6-7

A spiritual gift is given to each
of us so we can help each other.

1 CORINTHIANS 12:7

Just as our bodies have many parts
and each part has a special function,
so it is with Christ's body. We are many parts
of one body, and we all belong to each other.

ROMANS 12:4-5

Now you have every spiritual gift
you need as you eagerly wait for
the return of our Lord Jesus Christ.

1 CORINTHIANS 1:7

81

Let love be your highest goal!
But you should also desire
the special abilities the Spirit gives.

1 CORINTHIANS 14:1

Every good and perfect gift is
from above, coming down from the Father
of the heavenly lights, who does not
change like shifting shadows.

JAMES 1:17

God also testified to it by signs,
wonders and various miracles,
and by gifts of the Holy Spirit
distributed according to His will.

HEBREWS 2:4

When the
FRUIT of
your service
is out of all
proportion to
the GIFTS
you possess,
that is

blessing!

Watchman Nee

GraceNotes
of
Thanksgiving

Be thankful in all circumstances,
for this is God's will for you
who belong to Christ Jesus.

1 THESSALONIANS 5:18

Whatever you do in word or deed,
do all in the name of the Lord Jesus,
giving thanks to God the Father through Him.

COLOSSIANS 3:17

Give thanks to the LORD, for He is good!
His faithful love endures forever.

PSALM 136:1

Since we are receiving a kingdom that
cannot be shaken, let us be thankful,
and so worship God acceptably
with reverence and awe.

HEBREWS 12:28

Give thanks for everything to God the Father
in the name of our Lord Jesus Christ.

EPHESIANS 5:20

"Giving thanks is a sacrifice
that truly honors Me."

PSALM 50:23

The LORD is my strength and shield.
I trust Him with all my heart. He helps me,
and my heart is filled with joy.
I burst out in songs of thanksgiving.

PSALM 28:7

Let us come before Him with thanksgiving
and extol Him with music and song.

PSALM 95:2

Enter into His gates with thanksgiving,
and into His courts with praise.
Be thankful to Him, and bless His name.

PSALM 100:4

Give thanks to the LORD
and proclaim His greatness.
Let the whole world know
what He has done.

1 CHRONICLES 16:8

Gratitude
changes
the pangs of
MEMORY into
a tranquil JOY.

Dietrich Bonhoeffer

You made all the delicate,
inner parts of my body and knit me together
in my mother's womb. Thank You for making me so
wonderfully complex! Your workmanship
is marvelous – how well I know it.

PSALM 139:13-14

We give thanks to You, O God, we give thanks!
For Your wondrous works declare
that Your name is near.

PSALM 75:1

I will give thanks to the LORD with my whole heart;
I will recount all of Your wonderful deeds.
I will be glad and exult in You; I will sing praise
to Your name, O Most High.

PSALM 9:1-2

You are my God, and I will give thanks to You;
You are my God; I will extol You.

PSALM 118:28

Yours, LORD, is the greatness and the power
and the glory and the majesty and the splendor,
for everything in heaven and earth is Yours.
Yours, LORD, is the kingdom; You are exalted
as head over all. Now, our God, we give You thanks,
and praise Your glorious name.

1 CHRONICLES 29:11, 13

Thanks be to God for His indescribable gift!

2 CORINTHIANS 9:15

I will give to the LORD the thanks due
to His righteousness, and I will sing praise
to the name of the LORD, the Most High.

PSALM 7:17

I thank You for answering my prayer
and giving me victory!

PSALM 118:21

The Lord is good to everyone.
He showers compassion on all His creation.
All of Your works will thank You, Lord,
and Your faithful followers will praise You.

PSALM 145:9-10

Devote yourselves to prayer
with an alert mind and a thankful heart.

COLOSSIANS 4:2

A state of mind
that sees God
in everything is
evidence of growth
in **GRACE** and a

thankful heart.

Charles Finney

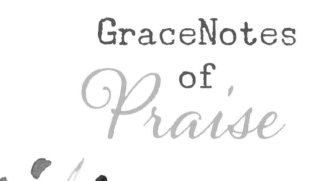

GraceNotes
of
Praise

Sing praises to God and to His name!
Sing loud praises to Him who rides the clouds.
His name is the LORD – rejoice in His presence!

PSALM 68:4

Praise be to the LORD God, the God of Israel,
who alone does marvelous deeds.
Praise be to His glorious name forever;
may the whole earth be filled with His glory.

PSALM 72:18-19

Let them praise the name of the LORD,
for His name alone is exalted;
His majesty is above earth and heaven.

PSALM 148:13

Praise the LORD! Sing to the LORD a new song.
Sing His praises in the assembly of the faithful.

PSALM 149:1

Declare His glory among the nations,
His wonders among all peoples. For the LORD
is great and greatly to be praised;
He is also to be feared above all gods.

1 CHRONICLES 16:24-25

Let heaven and earth praise Him,
the seas and all that move in them.

PSALM 69:34

O LORD, You are my God. I will exalt You, I will praise Your
name, for You have done wonderful things;
Your counsels of old are faithfulness and truth.

ISAIAH 25:1

Praise Him, you highest heavens,
and you waters above the heavens!
Let them praise the name of the LORD!
For He commanded and they were created.

PSALM 148:4-5

A Song of Praise

Praise the LORD. Praise the LORD,
you His servants; praise the name of the LORD.
Let the name of the LORD be praised,
both now and forevermore. From the rising
of the sun to the place where it sets,
the name of the LORD is to be praised.

PSALM 113:1-3

Praise the LORD, for the LORD is good;
sing praises to His name, for it is pleasant.

PSALM 135:3

When God does it,
we do more than
REMEMBER it, we
celebrate it.

Woodrow Kroll

Come, let us worship and bow down.
Let us kneel before the LORD our maker,
for He is our God. We are the people
He watches over, the flock under His care.

PSALM 95:6-7

"The hour is coming, and now is, when the true
worshipers will worship the Father in spirit
and truth; for the Father is seeking such to
worship Him. God is Spirit, and those who
worship Him must worship in spirit and truth."

JOHN 4:23-24

Exalt the LORD our God,
and worship at His holy mountain in Jerusalem,
for the LORD our God is holy!

PSALM 99:9

Give to the LORD glory and strength.
Give to the LORD the glory due His name;
bring an offering, and come before Him.
Oh, worship the LORD in the beauty of holiness!
Tremble before Him, all the earth.

1 CHRONICLES 16:28-30

Therefore, I urge you, brothers and sisters,
in view of God's mercy, to offer your bodies
as a living sacrifice, holy and pleasing to God –
this is your true and proper worship.

ROMANS 12:1

Let us go to the sanctuary of the LORD;
let us worship at the footstool of His throne.

PSALM 132:7

Give unto the Lord the glory due to His name;
worship the Lord in the beauty of holiness.

PSALM 29:2

Exalt the Lord our God;
worship at His footstool! Holy is He!

PSALM 99:5

Jesus said to him, "Away from Me, Satan!
For it is written: 'Worship the Lord your God,
and serve Him only.'"

MATTHEW 4:10

A true love
for God must begin
with a delight in
HIS HOLINESS.
Jonathan Edwards

GraceNotes
of
Salvation

"I have blotted out, like a thick cloud,
your transgressions, and like a cloud, your sins.
Return to Me, for I have redeemed you."

ISAIAH 44:22

As far as the east is from the west,
so far has He removed
our transgressions from us.

PSALM 103:12

"I will forgive their wickedness, and
I will never again remember their sins."

HEBREWS 8:12

Though your sins are like scarlet, they shall be as
white as snow; though they are red as crimson,
they shall be like wool.

ISAIAH 1:18

The Lord our God is merciful and forgiving.

DANIEL 9:9

He took a cup, and when He had
given thanks He gave it to them, saying,
"Drink of it, all of you, for this is My blood
of the covenant, which is poured out
for many for the forgiveness of sins."

MATTHEW 26:27-28

All the prophets testify about Him
that everyone who believes in Him receives
forgiveness of sins through His name.

ACTS 10:43

Now there is no condemnation
for those who belong to Christ Jesus.
And because you belong to Him,
the power of the life-giving Spirit has freed
you from the power of sin that leads to death.

ROMANS 8:1-2

If anyone sins, we have an Advocate with the Father,
Jesus Christ the righteous. And He Himself is the
propitiation for our sins, and not for ours only
but also for the whole world.

1 JOHN 2:1-2

We praise God for the glorious grace He
has poured out on us who belong to His dear Son.
He is so rich in kindness and grace
that He purchased our freedom with the blood of
His Son and forgave our sins.

EPHESIANS 1:6-7

He has delivered us from the domain
of darkness and transferred us to
the kingdom of His beloved Son, in whom we have
redemption, the forgiveness of sins.

COLOSSIANS 1:13-14

After grief
for sin there
should be
JOY for
forgiveness.

A. W. Pink

To each one of us grace has been
given as Christ apportioned it.

EPHESIANS 4:7

"My grace is sufficient for you,
for My power is made perfect in weakness."

2 CORINTHIANS 12:9

Let us then approach God's throne
of grace with confidence, so that we may
receive mercy and find grace
to help us in our time of need.

HEBREWS 4:16

God saved you by His grace when you believed.
And you can't take credit for this;
it is a gift from God.

EPHESIANS 2:8

God is able to make all grace
abound to you, so that having all sufficiency
in all things at all times,
you may abound in every good work.

2 CORINTHIANS 9:8

Sin is no longer your master,
for you no longer live under the
requirements of the law. Instead,
you live under the freedom of God's grace.

ROMANS 6:14

Through Him we have also obtained access
by faith into this grace in which we stand,
and we rejoice in hope of the glory of God.

ROMANS 5:2

From His abundance we have all received
one gracious blessing after another.

JOHN 1:16

The LORD is compassionate and gracious,
slow to anger, abounding in love.

PSALM 103:8

For the grace of God has appeared,
bringing salvation for all people.

TITUS 2:11

We are all saved the same way,
by the undeserved grace of the Lord Jesus.

ACTS 15:11

I commend you to God and to the word
of His grace, which is able to build you up
and to give you the inheritance among
all those who are sanctified.

ACTS 20:32

As
grace
is first
from God, so it
is continually from
Him, as much as
light is all day
long from the sun,
as well as
at first dawn or
at sunrising.
Jonathan Edwards

"Whoever believes has eternal life."

JOHN 6:47

"Everyone who lives in Me and
believes in Me will never ever die."

JOHN 11:26

Whoever has the Son has life;
whoever does not have the Son
of God does not have life.

1 JOHN 5:12

"My Father's will is that everyone
who looks to the Son and believes in Him
shall have eternal life, and I will raise
them up at the last day."

JOHN 6:40

For the wages of sin is death,
but the free gift of God is eternal life
through Christ Jesus our Lord.

ROMANS 6:23

"Indeed, the time is coming when all the dead in their graves will hear the voice of God's Son, and they will rise again. Those who have done good will rise to experience eternal life, and those who have continued in evil will rise to experience judgment."

JOHN 5:28-29

"I give them eternal life, and they shall never perish; no one will snatch them out of My hand. My Father, who has given them to Me, is greater than all; no one can snatch them out of My Father's hand. I and the Father are one."

JOHN 10:28-30

He who believes in the Son has everlasting life; and he who does not believe the Son shall not see life, but the wrath of God abides on him.

JOHN 3:36

I write these things to you who believe
in the name of the Son of God so that
you may know that you have eternal life.

1 JOHN 5:13

"You can enter God's Kingdom only through
the highway to hell is broad,
and its gate is wide for the many who choose
that way. But the gateway to life is
very narrow and the road is difficult,
and only a few ever find it."

MATTHEW 7:13-14

"Whoever drinks of this water will thirst again,
but whoever drinks of the water that I shall
give him will never thirst. But the water that
I shall give him will become in him a fountain
of water springing up into everlasting life."

JOHN 4:13-14

Your actions,
in passing,
pass not away,
for every
GOOD WORK
is a grain of
seed for
eternal life.

Bernard of Clairvaux

GraceNotes
of
Encouragement

A friend is always a friend.

PROVERBS 17:17

Two are better than one, because they have a good reward for their labor. For if they fall, one will lift up his companion. Though one may be overpowered by another, two can withstand him. And a threefold cord is not quickly broken.

ECCLESIASTES 4:9-10, 12

As iron sharpens iron,
so a friend sharpens a friend.

PROVERBS 27:17

Share each other's burdens,
and in this way obey the law of Christ.

GALATIANS 6:2

Perfume and incense bring joy to the heart,
and the pleasantness of a friend springs
from their heartfelt advice.

PROVERBS 27:9

Walk with the wise and become wise;
associate with fools and get in trouble.

PROVERBS 13:20

Don't befriend angry people or associate
with hot-tempered people, or you will learn
to be like them and endanger your soul.

PROVERBS 22:24-25

Where there is no guidance, a people falls,
but in an abundance of counselors there is safety.

PROVERBS 11:14

There are "friends" who destroy each other,
but a real friend sticks closer than a brother.

PROVERBS 18:24

"No longer do I call you servants, for the servant does
not know what his master is doing; but I have called you
friends, for all that I have heard from My Father I have
made known to you."

JOHN 15:15

The friendship of the LORD is for those
who fear Him, and He makes known
to them His covenant.

PSALM 25:14

Friendship
is born at that
moment when one
person says to
another:
"What! You too?
I thought I was
the only one."
C. S. Lewis

Let your conversation be always full of grace,
seasoned with salt, so that you may
know how to answer everyone.

COLOSSIANS 4:6

"It's not what goes into your mouth
that defiles you; you are defiled by the words
that come out of your mouth."

MATTHEW 15:11

Let no corrupting talk come out
of your mouths, but only such as
is good for building up, as fits the occasion,
that it may give grace to those who hear.

EPHESIANS 4:29

A gentle answer turns away wrath,
but a harsh word stirs up anger.

PROVERBS 15:1

A wholesome tongue is a tree of life,
but perverseness in it breaks the spirit.

PROVERBS 15:4

Gracious words are a honeycomb,
sweet to the soul and healing to the bones.

PROVERBS 16:24

The words of the godly are
a life-giving fountain; the words of
the wicked conceal violent intentions.

PROVERBS 10:11

The lips of the godly speak helpful words,
but the mouth of the wicked
speaks perverse words.

PROVERBS 10:32

Let the words of my mouth
and the meditation of my heart be
acceptable in Your sight, O Lord,
my strength and my Redeemer.

PSALM 19:14

Whatever you do or say,
do it as a representative
of the Lord Jesus, giving thanks
through Him to God the Father.

COLOSSIANS 3:17

Kind words
do not cost much.
Yet they
ACCOMPLISH much.

Blaise Pascal